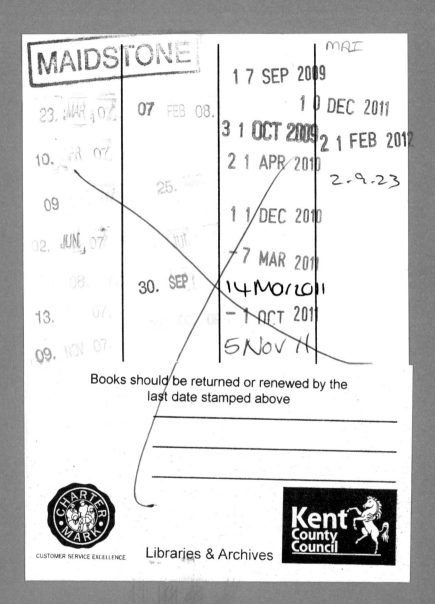

Super Senses

Seeing

Mary Mackill

www.raintreepublishers.co.uk

Visit our website to find out more information about **Raintree** books.

To order:

☎ Phone 44 (0) 1865 888112

🗎 Send a fax to 44 (0) 1865 314091

💻 Visit the Raintree Bookshop at **www.raintreepublishers.co.uk** to browse our catalogue and order online.

First published in Great Britain by Raintree, Halley Court, Jordan Hill, Oxford OX2 8EJ, part of Harcourt Education.
Raintree is a registered trademark of Harcourt Education Ltd.

Editorial: Kate Bellamy
Design: Jo Hinton-Malivoire and bigtop
Illustrations: Darren Lingard
Picture Research: Hannah Taylor and Fiona Orbell
Production: Helen McCreath

Originated by Chroma Graphics (Overseas) Pte. Ltd
Printed and bound in China by
South China Printing Company

ISBN 1 406 20020 4 (hardback)
10 09 08 07 06
10 9 8 7 6 5 4 3 2 1

ISBN 1 406 20027 1 (paperback)
11 10 09 08 07
10 9 8 7 6 5 4 3 2 1

British Library Cataloguing in Publication Data
Mackill, Mary
Seeing – (Super Senses)
612.8'4
A full catalogue record for this book is available from the British Library.

Acknowledgements
The publishers would like to thank the following for permission to reproduce photographs:
Alamy Images pp. **5** (Dynamic Graphics Group), **15**, **23d** (Imagestate), **9**; ARDEA p. **19** (C. McDougal); Corbis pp. **16** (royalty free), **21**, **22** (Gavriel Jecan), **4**, **23c** (Randy Faris), **6** (Tom & Dee Ann McCarthy), **18** (William Manning); Digital Vision pp. **14**, **23a**; Getty Images pp. **10**, **13** (Photodisc), **7**, **11**, **12**, **23b** (Stone), **17** (Stone +); Harcourt Education Ltd pp. **20t**, **20b** (Tudor Photography).

Cover photograph reproduced with permission of Superstock/Pixtal.

Every effort has been made to contact copyright holders of any material reproduced in this book. Any omissions will be rectified in subsequent printings if notice is given to the publishers.

The paper used to print this book comes from sustainable resources.

Contents

Some words are shown in bold, **like this**. They are explained in the glossary on page 23.

What are my senses?

You have five **senses**. They help you see, hear, taste, smell and touch things.

Pretend you are at a funfair.

What can you see?

Seeing is one of your five senses.

What do I use to see?

You use your eyes and brain to see.

Your eyes need light to see objects.

pupil

eye

Each eye has a special hole in the middle. This is called the **pupil**.

The pupil lets light into the eye.

How do I see?

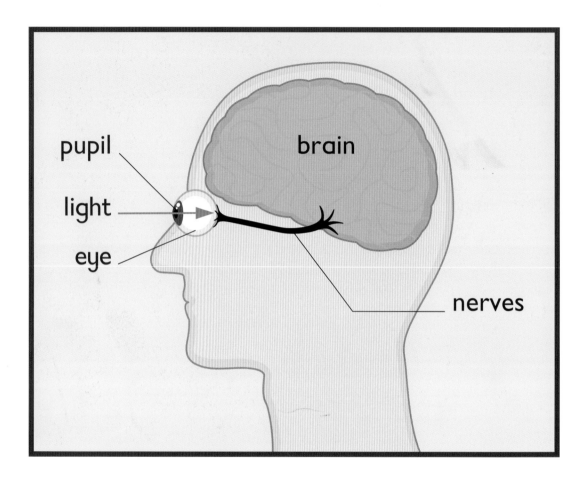

When light comes into your **pupil** it hits some **nerves**.

The nerves send a message to your brain.

Your brain picks up the message.

Your brain would tell you that this ball is coming towards you!

What can I see?

Your eyes can see lots of colours.

Your eyes can see different shapes and sizes, too.

What shapes can you see here?

How does seeing help me?

Seeing helps you to stay safe.

You can see cars and stay out of their way.

Seeing helps you to work out how close something is.

What can help me to see better?

A **magnifying glass** makes small things look bigger.

A **telescope** makes things that are far away look closer.

How can I look after my eyes?

Your eyes are important.

Without them, you could not read this book!

Give your eyes lots of rest.

Try not to look at a television screen for too long.

Animals can see too!

Some animals use their **sense** of sight to find food.

Some animals, like this tiger, can see well in the dark.

Test your sense of sight

This boy can see only a small part of the picture.

When you see all of something, it is easier to tell what it is.

Can you see what this is?

Turn over the page to find out.

Seeing is super!

Your **sense** of sight:

- tells you what colour, shape, and size something is

- warns you if danger is near

- helps you to read this book!

Glossary

 **magnifying glass** glass object that makes small things look bigger

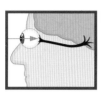 **nerves** parts inside your body. Nerves work with the brain to sense things.

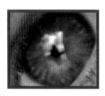 **pupil** hole in the middle of your eye that lets in light

 **sense** something that helps you to see, touch, taste, smell, and hear the things around you

 **telescope** large object that makes things that are far away look closer

Index

Note to Parents and Teachers

Reading for information is an important part of a child's literacy development. Learning begins with a question about something. Help children think of themselves as investigators and researchers by encouraging their questions about the world around them. Each chapter in this book begins with a question. Read the question together. Look at the pictures. Talk about what you think the answer might be. Then read the text to find out if your predictions were correct. Think of other questions you could ask about the topic, and discuss where you might find the answers. Assist children in using the picture glossary and the index to practice new vocabulary and research skills.